WHAT I THINK
I WANT TO BE

WHAT I THINK I WANT TO BE

LAURIE S. HURT

LitPrime
"Your story is our priority"

LitPrime Solutions
21250 Hawthorne Blvd
Suite 500, Torrance, CA 90503
www.litprime.com
Phone: 1-800-981-9893

Published by LitPrime Solutions   03/06/2023

ISBN: 979-8-88703-165-1(sc)
ISBN: 979-8-88703-166-8(hc)
ISBN: 979-8-88703-167-5(e)

Library of Congress Control Number: 2023902918

Dedication

This book is dedicated first of all to God,
for without God I could not have completed this.

It is also dedicated to my eldest brother, who died March
1999 of Leukemia, and to my parents, sister, and brother,
children, grandchildren, nieces, and nephews.

And it is dedicated especially to my granddaughter,
born this year.

As I got up and looked around me,
I was thinking what I would
like to be:

An Astronaut

who explores space,
who sends back samples of a
whole new place, or someone who
walks way out on the moon
and puts information together,
to be developed soon.

As I got up and looked around me,
I was thinking what I would
like to be:

A Bank Teller

Seems to be just right,
Completely right for me;
Someone who greets customers
and smiles with glee,
and counts out money,
and adds on an adding machine.

As I got up and looked around me,
I was thinking what I would
like to be:

A Doctor

Is what I would like to be,
a person who cares and helps
others during emergencies,
a person who gives out shots,
and sometimes maybe lollipops,
this could help especially.

As I got up and looked around me,
I was thinking what I would
like to be:

An Engineer

is what I would like to be,
someone who builds bridges and
draws pictures and designs
buildings so easily.

As I got up and looked around me,
I was thinking what I would
like to be:

A Lawyer

who settles arguments,
a lawyer who knows
right from wrong,
a lawyer who talks to the judges
about people who they do wrong.

As I got up and looked around me,
I was thinking what I would
like to be:

A Mail Person

who sells stamps and
money orders, you see,
and handles a lot of
special deliveries.

As I got up and looked around me,
I was thinking what I would
like to be:

A Teacher

who gives out homework
and study sheets, and can help you
understand the importance of life
more abundantly.

Of all the things I want to do,
I must first of all finish school,
and believe in myself-
that will be the golden rule.

Remember to set your goals,

work for that diploma or degree,

keep your mind on the future,

and always believe that this can be the

key to your life in order to succeed.